はい Hai! 3

Coursebook

My かぞく!

Sue Burnham and Michael Sedunary

Heinemann

Heinemann

An imprint of Pearson Education Australia
A division of Pearson Australia Group Pty Ltd
20 Thackray Road, Port Melbourne, Victoria 3207
PO Box 460, Port Melbourne, Victoria 3207
www.pearsoned.com.au/schools

Copyright © Pearson Education Australia 2008 (a division of Pearson Australia Group Pty Ltd)
First published 2003 by Heinemann
2011   2010   2009   2008
8   7   6   5   4

Reproduction and communication for educational purposes
The Australian *Copyright Act 1968* (the Act) allows a maximum of one chapter or 10% of this book, whichever is the greater, to be copied by any educational institution for its educational purposes provided that that educational institution (or the body that administers it) has given a remuneration notice to Copyright Agency Limited (CAL) under the Act.

For details of the CAL licence for educational institutions contact Copyright Agency Limited (www.copyright.com.au).

Reproduction and communication for other purposes
Except as permitted under the Act, for example any fair dealing for the purposes of study, research, criticism or review, no part of this book may be reproduced, stored in a retrieval system, or transmitted in any form or by any means without prior written permission. All enquiries should be made to the publisher at the address above.

This book is not to be treated as a blackline master; that is, any photocopying beyond fair dealing requires prior written permission.

Commissioning Editor: Catriona McKenzie
Editor: Tina Hutchings with assistance from Anne Gugger
Designer: Sue Dani
Cover illustration: st2creative
Illustrations: Tomomi Sarafov, st2creative, Sue Dani and Peter Townsend
Photography by Michael Sedunary
Teaching consultant: Diane Furusho
Language consultant: Matt Hagino
Proofreader: Jude Hunter

Film supplied by Splitting Image
Printed in China by Wing King Tong Co. Ltd.

National Library of Australia cataloguing-in-publication data:

Burnham, Sue
  Hai! 3 : coursebook.

  For secondary school students aged 13–14 years.
  ISBN 978 1 74085 013 1.

  1. Japanese language – Textbooks for foreign speakers –
  English – Juvenile literature. I. Sedunary, Michael
  II. Title.

495.68

Pearson Australia Group Pty Ltd   ABN 40 004 245 943

Acknowledgements
The authors would like to thank the Oota family and Akira Otsuka for their assistance in Japan.

Photograph on page 26 courtesy of Japan National Tourist Organisation.

Every effort has been made to trace and acknowledge copyright. The publisher would welcome any information from people who believe they own copyright to material in this book.

Contents

Introduction ... iv

だい 1 か　All in the family ... 1

TOPICS

My family
At home in Japan

まんが：きょうこさんの かぞく

LANGUAGE AND SCRIPT

- Counting people 一人、二人、三人、etc.
- How many people are in your family?
  ごかぞくは 何人 ですか。
- There are ~ in my family かぞくは～人 です。
- The people in my family ちち、はは、あに、etc.
- What they are into ～はよく～
- Kanji 人、何

だい 2 か　Whatever you like ... 15

TOPICS

Likes and dislikes
My family – extended
Some special days in Japan
Bath time

まんが：父の日

LANGUAGE AND SCRIPT

- Likes ～が大すき、すき、まあまあ すき
- Dislikes ～があまり、すきじゃない
- Speaking to and about family members
  お父さん、お母さん、etc.
- Kanji 父、母
- New readings 大、日

だい 3 か　Time out! ... 33

TOPICS

More time
さようなら roomaji

LANGUAGE AND SCRIPT

- Telling the time: 5 minutes ～時5分、15分、etc.
- Telling the time: 10 minutes ～時10分、20分 etc.
- Kanji 分、時、半

だい 4 か　What a day! ... 40

TOPICS

Daily routine
Food and drink
Breakfast in Japan

まんが：じゃんけん！

LANGUAGE AND SCRIPT

- Daily routine:
  get up at … ～時に おきます
  go to bed at … ～時に ねます
  go to work/school at … ～時に～に 行きます
  get home at … ～時に うちに かえります
  have breakfast, a snack, dinner そして、
  ～を 食べます／のみます
- Breakfast foods みそしる、ごはん、
  さかな、etc.
- Kanji 食、校
- New reading 何

だい 5 か　Happy days! ... 57

TOPICS

Days of the week
When things are on
Visiting Hakone
Family presentation

うた：日曜日も

LANGUAGE AND SCRIPT

- What day is it today? きょうは 何曜日
  ですか。
- What day is it on? ～は 何曜日 ですか
- Kanji 月、火、水、木、金、土、曜
- New reading 日

Vocabulary list

Japanese–English ... 64

English–Japanese ... 66

Introduction

It's time to meet Kyouko Yamaguchi, the 'star' of **Hai! 3**. Kyouko introduces us to her karaoke-loving friend, Ritsuko Kawate, who will keep her company through most of the book.

The theme of this book is My かぞく; 'My family'. We will be spending a lot of time with きょうこさんの かぞく, including her mother, who hates cooking, and her little brother who thinks he's a Ninja. As Ritsuko says, おもしろい かぞく ですね!!

1 こんにちは！
わたしは 山口 きょうこ です。14さい です。

2 なつまちに すんで います。
わたしの うちは 小さい です。

3 ともだちの りつこさん です。

川手 りつこ です。
どうぞ よろしく。

しゅうまつに、わたしと りつこさんは まちに 行きます。

4 カラオケを します。
りつこさんは おもしろい ですね。

All in the family

だい1か

べんきょうページ (peeji)

Counting people

たんご

何人	なんにん nannin	how many people?
一人	ひとり hitori	
二人	ふたり futari	
三人	さんにん sannin	
四人	よにん yonin	
五人	ごにん gonin	

六人	ろくにん rokunin
七人	しちにん shichinin, ななにん nananin
八人	はちにん hachinin
九人	きゅうにん kyuunin, くにん kunin
十人	じゅうにん juunin

How many are there in your family?

ごかぞくは何人ですか。
gokazoku wa nannin desu ka.

五人です。
gonin desu.

There are three in my family

かぞくは三人です。
kazoku wa sannin desu.

In だい1か you will learn:

- to talk about your family
  – how many there are
  – who they are
  – what they're into
- to introduce family members
- to count people
- another word for 'I' (if you're a boy)
- to read and write the kanji 人 and 何
- how one kanji can have different readings
- about going home in Japan
  – what to say
  – what to do

かんじ

Time for some more fun with かんじ! Let's go back to the word 日本, the word for 'Japan'. You know that 本 means 'source' or 'origin' (of the sun). And you know that 本 also means 'book' (a *source* of knowledge and the *origin* of much learning). We like the idea that a かんじ can have more than one *meaning*, especially when we understand that the meanings are related.

Another great thing about かんじ is that one character can have more than one *reading*. Look at 一 and 二, for example. Until now you have always read them as いち *ichi* and に *ni*, but in this chapter you see these かんじ numbers in front of 人 and read them as ひと *hito* and ふた *futa*.

And what about 人, a new かんじ meaning 'person'? After 一 and 二 you read it as り *ri*, but after all the other かんじ numbers you read it as にん *nin*.

Don't you just love the idea that one character can have several different readings? It's all part of the mystery and the challenge of かんじ. But there is also something very simple about かんじ. Have another look at 一人. Could there be a simpler, clearer way of writing 'one person' – in any language?

person — 2 strokes

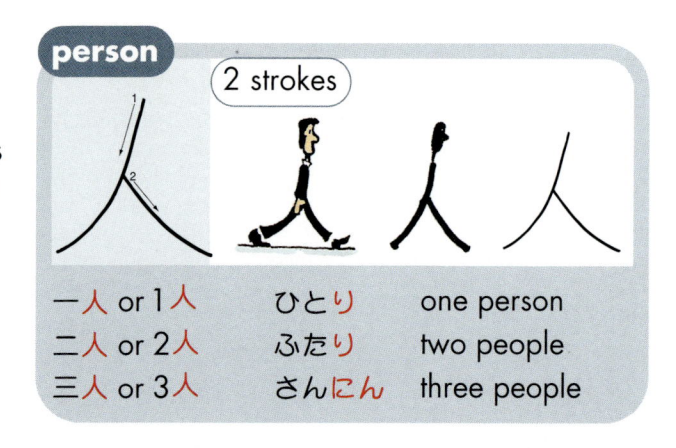

一人 or 1人	ひとり	one person
二人 or 2人	ふたり	two people
三人 or 3人	さんにん	three people

what? — 7 strokes

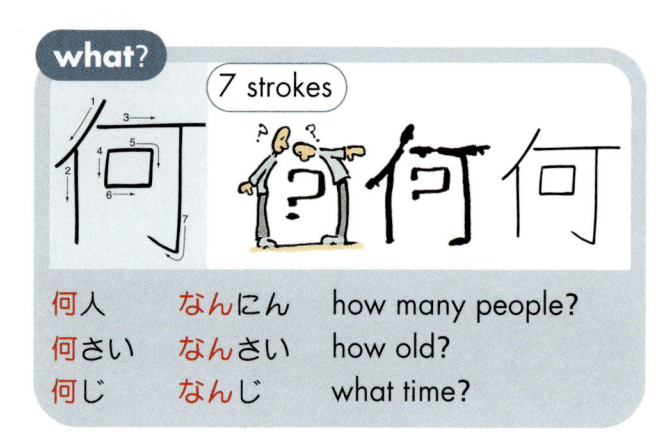

何人	なんにん	how many people?
何さい	なんさい	how old?
何じ	なんじ	what time?

しましょう

1. • Look at the labels on these sleepy, dopey, grumpy looking characters and work out what they and their friends are called in 日本語. (In this case you read 小 as こ.)

   • You know another reading of 小; what is it?

だい一か

しましょう

この グループは 何人 ですか。
（gu ru u pu）

2 If we tell you that この means 'this', you'll be able to work out what we're asking about this not-so-grumpy group.

3 Have you ever noticed that when people form a queue, each person in the line does something a little different while waiting?

Some read, some fidget, some talk on a mobile, some check the time … you get the idea.

See if you can build a line-up of people, one at a time, with each new arrival bringing a different activity to the group.

Count yourself in as you take your place in the queue and then demonstrate your individual waiting style.

五人。

Number of people in the family

▶ To ask someone how many people there are in their family, begin with the 'your family' word, ごかぞく, and then ask 何人 ですか.

　　ごかぞくは 何人 ですか。 *gokazoku wa nannin desu ka.*
　　How many people are in your family?

▶ To answer this question, say the number followed by 人.

　　五人 です。 *gonin desu.*
　　There are five.

▶ To say (without being asked) how many there are in your family, begin with the 'my family' word, かぞく, and then say the number followed by 人.

　　かぞくは 五人 です。 *kazoku wa gonin desu.*
　　There are five people in my family.

たんご		
	ごかぞく *gokazoku*	your family
	かぞく *kazoku*	my family

だい一か

3

口 れんしゅう

Family album 1

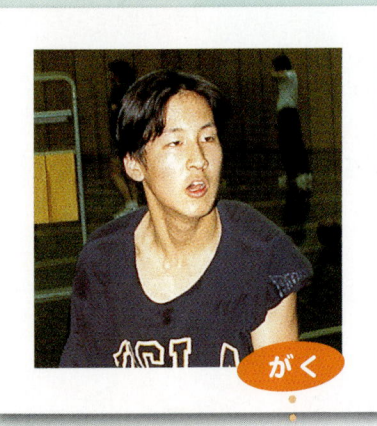

だい一か

がく

みえ

ようこ

ともみ

まさお

1. When your partner says a name, pretend to be the person in the picture and tell your partner how many people there are in your family.

   You will say something like this:

   かぞくは 5人 です。

2. Your partner will pretend to be each person in the photos above. When you ask them about the number of people in their family, they will be able to tell you by tracing the line to their 'family album'.

   Here is an example of the conversation you would have with がく:

   You: がくさん、ごかぞくは 何人 ですか。

   Partner: 5人 です。

べんきょうページ (peeji)

The people in your family

かぞくは ちちと ははと おとうとが 二人と わたし です。
kazoku wa chichi to haha to otouto ga futari to watashi desu.

かぞくは ははと ぼく です。
kazoku wa haha to boku desu

たんご

かぞく *kazoku*	my family	あに *ani*	my big brother
りょうしん *ryoushin*	my parents	あね *ane*	my big sister
ちち *chichi*	my father	おとうと *otouto*	my little brother
はは *haha*	my mother	いもうと *imouto*	my little sister
		ぼく *boku*	I (boy speaking)

しましょう

たんご tennis

You and a classmate can play 'たんご tennis' by serving and returning words from any たんご list. The aim of the game is to keep a rally going for as long as possible. You have played the perfect rally when you have used all the words in the たんご list you are using.

Here are a couple of examples of 'たんご tennis' you could play with words from this chapter.

- You serve a 'family' word in 日本語 and your classmate returns with the 'family' word for the opposite sex. You serve ちち, your classmate returns はは. Now you're at the net and volley with あに …

- Your classmate serves a 'family' word in 日本語 and you use a double-handed backhand return: you give the translation in えい語 and then another 'family' word in 日本語.

  Your classmate serves ちち, you return 'my father', plus はは. Your classmate returns 'my mother', plus …

だい一か

The people in your family

▶ After saying how many people are in your family you usually go on to say who they are. To do this, use the appropriate words from the 'my family' list, join them together with と and add yourself at the end.

> ちちと ははと いもうとと わたし です。
> *chichi to haha to imouto to watashi desu.*
> There is my dad, my mum, my little sister and me.

▶ If you haven't started off by saying how many there are, you need to begin with the 'my family' word, かぞく *kazoku*. Instead of ちちと はは *chichi to haha*, you can use the word りょうしん *ryoushin*, which means 'my parents'.

> かぞくは りょうしんと おとうとと わたし です。
> *kazoku wa ryoushin to otouto to watashi desu.*
> In my family there's my parents, my little brother and me.

▶ If you are a boy, you can say ぼく *boku* instead of わたし when you are talking about yourself. ぼく is a bit more casual than わたし and girls just don't say it. Boys can still say わたし if they want to.

> かぞくは ちちと ははと あねと ぼく です。
> *kazoku wa chichi to haha to ane to boku desu.*
> My family is (made up of) Dad, Mum, my big sister and me.

▶ If you have more than one brother or sister say (family member) が *ga* (number).

> かぞくは いもうとが 二人と わたし です。
> *kazoku wa imouto ga futari to watashi desu.*
> In my family there's two younger sisters and me.

▶ It's hard to give an English translation of words like あに. It does mean 'my older brother', but this sounds pretty formal so sometimes we call him 'my big brother'. Even this isn't quite right because usually, when we're talking about a brother, big or little, we simply call him 'my brother'.

口れんしゅう

Family album II

- With a partner, take it in turns to be わたし or ぼく in each family photo.
- When it's your turn to be わたし or ぼく, you have to answer your partner's question: ごかぞくは 何人 ですか。
- You will find a couple of possible answers written next to your family photo, so you have to choose the right one. If you're not sure which answer to choose, have a closer look at the photo.

1 ぼく

二人 です。 ちち / はは と ぼく です。

2 わたし

三人 / 四人 です。ちちと ははと わたし です。

3 わたし

五人 / 四人 です。ちちと ははと あに / あね と わたし です。

4 ぼく

五人 / 七人 です。 ちち / りょうしん と あに / あね と いもうと / おとうと と ぼく / わたし です。

Extended family

Now that you can say who is in your family, as well as how many people there are in your family, why not go back to **Family Album I** on page 4 and *extend* the conversations that you had there? Your aim is to have conversations like the ones you have just been having here. (Before you start talking, spend some time with your partner working out who's who in each family.) You are the 'shady figure' in your family.

だい一か

I'm home!

In Japan, when people get home they open the front door and call out to whoever is inside the house, ただいま! This is more than a casual 'I'm home', that you might or might not call out according to your mood. It is a set phrase that people always use when they get home.

Often these set phrases require a set response. For example, the person inside the house is not free to yell out any old expression of welcome, but always replies おかえりなさい.

When you come into someone else's home as a visitor, you don't say ただいま; your set phrase is おじゃまします, which means something like 'Don't mind me'.

たたみ room with a こたつ

げんかん

When you visit a Japanese house, your first port of call is the げんかん. The げんかん is a porch-like entrance area, and although it is inside the front door it is still regarded as part of the outside world. It is here that you take off your shoes and put on a pair of 'inside' slippers. You'll find them on the 'inside' floor, a step up from the げんかん floor. As a visitor, you'll be shown a pair of slippers that you can put on.

For Japanese people this footwear swapping is a part of everyday life, so they sensibly avoid shoes with complicated lacing systems. They are also careful not to go visiting with holes in their socks! As a visitor to Japan you may sometimes find it quite a challenge to keep your balance while you remember to avoid putting a slippered foot down onto the げんかん floor, or keep from putting your foot up onto the 'inside' floor while you still have your shoe on!

Japanese homes often have a room that has straw mats called たたみ on the floor. When they go into the たたみ room, Japanese people take off their slippers. If the たたみ room has a こたつ they don't have to worry about getting cold feet. A こたつ is a low table with an electric foot-warmer underneath. It's a great place for the family to feel snug on a cold winter's night.

The other time you may take off your slippers inside is when you go the toilet. In many homes there are special toilet slippers that are used only for that room. You'll certainly raise some Japanese eyebrows if you forget to change out of your toilet (WC) slippers and start tramping around the kitchen in them!

When Japanese people leave the house they reverse the process described earlier: in the げんかん they change from slippers into shoes and announce that they are going by saying: いってきます. Whoever is staying at home knows what to say in response: いってらっしゃい – 'Off you go, then, see you when you get back'.

だい一か

Cultural Miss

Now it's time to meet Maggie McGaffe who was recently awarded the title of this year's Cultural Miss. Her prize is a visit to Japan where she will practise the language of the country and experience its culture.

Your job is to keep an eye on Maggie to see how she is going. Whenever you see her, observe what she is doing and judge whether she is living up to her title, Cultural Miss. Here is your first chance.

べんきょうページ (peeji)

Introducing your family

1. いもうと です。なまえは きょうこ です。
imouto desu. namae wa Kyouko desu.

2. いもうとの へや です。
imouto no heya desu.
いもうとは よく かいものに 行きます。
imouto wa yoku kaimono ni ikimasu.

Introducing your family

▶ To introduce a person in your family, say how they are related to you and then give their name.

あに です。なまえは じゅん です。*ani desu. namae wa Jun desu.*
This is my older brother. His name is Jun.

▶ There is also a 'shorthand' introduction formula, similar to the one you used for introducing a friend.

あにの じゅん です。*ani no Jun desu.*
This is my older brother, Jun.

What are they into?

You have already seen よく, meaning 'well', in the expression よく できました. Well done!

よく also means 'often' and you can use it when you want to say that someone is really 'into' something. Just put よく before the thing they often do.

ははは よく かいものに 行きます。*haha wa yoku kaimono ni ikimasu.*
Mum often goes shopping. (Mum is really into shopping.)

あには よく スポーツを します。*ani wa yoku supootsu o shimasu.* (su po o tsu)
My (older) brother plays a lot of sport. (My brother is really into sport.)

たんご

へや	*heya*	room
よく	*yoku*	often

だい一か

口 れんしゅう

なまえ：みえこ	なまえ：みなこ	なまえ：さわこ	なまえ：まさる	なまえ：ふじお
何さい？：41	何さい？：10	何さい？：13	何さい？：15	何さい？：45
しゅうまつに…： 	しゅうまつに…： 	しゅうまつに…： 	しゅうまつに…： 	しゅうまつに…： 

Part 1

- Choose to be either まさる or さわこ and introduce yourself.
- Say how old you are and what you are into on the weekend. (Check the たんご box for any verbs that you may have forgotten.)
- Introduce your family by saying how many people there are in it …
- … and who they are.

If you were pretending to be みなこ this is what you would say:

わたしは みなこ です。

10さい です。

しゅうまつに、よく テレビ を 見ます。
(te re bi)

かぞくは 5人 です。

ちちと ははと あにと あねと わたし です。

Part 2

- Decide which two family members you are going to introduce individually.
- Say how each is related to you, how old they are and what they are into on the weekend.

For example, this is how you would introduce your 'father'.

ちちの ふじお です。

45さい です。

しゅうまつに、ちちは よく CDを ききます。

たんご

| ききます | 見ます |
| します | よみます |

だい一か

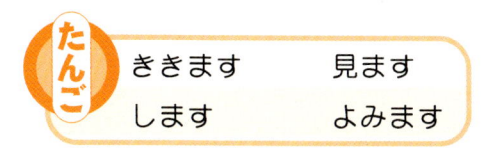

11

きょうこさんの かぞく

だい一か

1. ただいま！ / おじゃまします。
2. おかえりなさい。
3. はは です。
4. きょうこさん、ごかぞくは 何人 ですか。 / 五人 です。ははと... / Shhh! しずかに。
5. はははは よく テレビ を 見ます。 / ああ、おもしろい！
6. どうぞ。 / ありがとう ございます。
7. わたしの へやは... / こわい！ / あああ！
8. おとうとの ゆきお です。おとうとは にんじゃ です。 / へえ。
9. ゆきおさんは おもしろい ですね。

10. ゆきおの へや です。

11. 見て！きたない ですね。

12. ゆきおさんは 何さい ですか。
9さい です。

13. ああ、くさい です。

14.

15. あにの じゅんの へや です。うるさい です。

16. じゅんさんは 何さい ですか。
17さい です。

17. わたしの へや です。

18. きょうこさんは よく かいものに 行きますね。

19. 何ですか。ああ、「まゆみ」の CD ですね。

20. はい、カラオケ(ka ra o ke)の CD です。

21. うわあ！カラオケ(ka ra o ke)？ すごい！

だい一か

たんご			
ただいま	I'm home	くさい	smelly
おじゃまします	Don't mind me	テイクアウトの〜	takeaway ...
おかえりなさい	Welcome home	ピザ	pizza

1. How many people are there in きょうこ's family?
2. What do we learn about each person?
3. How does きょうこ describe her brothers?
4. In which frames do we see the げんかん of the house?

Whatever you like

だい 2 か

べんきょうページ (pe e ji) 🔘

Do you like it?

Yes, I love it

チョコレートが すき ですか。
(cho ko re e to)
chokoreeto ga suki desu ka.

はい、大すき です。
(だい)
hai, daisuki desu.

1

Yes, I like it

すしが すき ですか。
sushi ga suki desu ka.

はい、すき です。
hai, suki desu.

2

It's OK

チョコレートが すき ですか。
(cho ko re e to)
chokoreeto ga suki desu ka.

まあまあ すき です。
maamaa suki desu.

3

No, not much …

れんしゅうが すき ですか。
renshuu ga suki desu ka.

いいえ、あまり…（すきじゃない です。）
iie, amari … (suki janai desu).

4

In だい2か you will learn:

- to say what you like and don't like
- to ask others about what they like
- to ask others about their family
- to read and write the kanji 父 and 母
- a new way of reading 大 and 日
- which are the most popular animals in your class
- about some special days in Japan
- the 'do's and don'ts' of bath time

べんきょうページ

I like it

わたしは ぎゅうにゅうが すき です。
watashi wa gyuunyuu ga suki desu.

Shin likes it, Ken doesn't

けん

しん

しんさんは ジョギング が すき です。
Shinsan wa jogingu ga suki desu.

けんさんは ジョギング が すきじゃない です。
Kensan wa jogingu ga suki janai desu.

たんご — Some things to like or dislike

ケーキ (*keeki*)	cake
ぎゅうにゅう *gyuunyuu*	milk
にく *niku*	meat
すし *sushi*	sushi
ジョギング (*jogingu*)	jogging
すいえい *suiei*	swimming
れんしゅう *renshuu*	practice, training
しゅくだい *shukudai*	homework
そうじ *souji*	cleaning
サッカーの れんしゅう (*sakkaa*)	soccer practice
日本語の しゅくだい	Japanese homework
えい語の しゅくだい	English homework

だい二か

十六

Likes and dislikes – the question

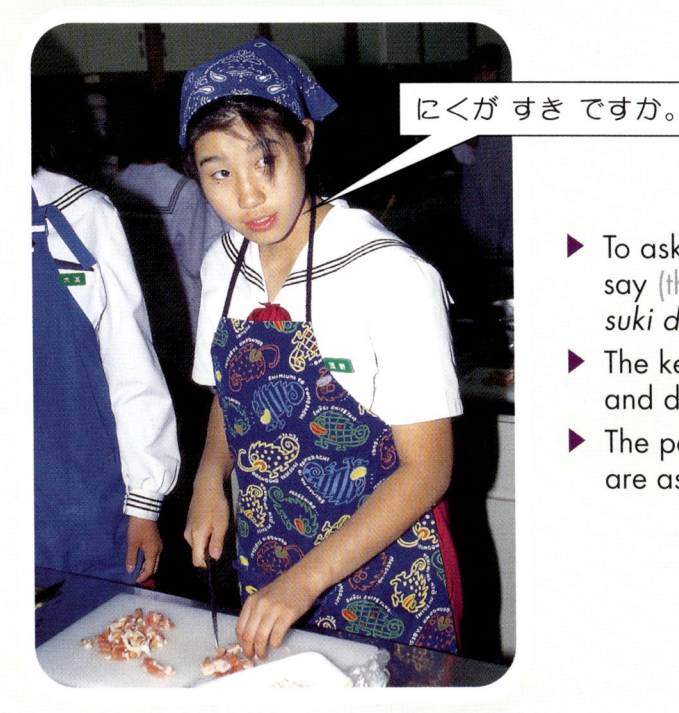

にくが すき ですか。

- To ask someone if they like something, say (thing) が すき ですか。 (thing) *ga suki desu ka*.
- The key word for talking about likes and dislikes is すき *suki*.
- The particle が *ga* follows the thing you are asking about.

Likes and dislikes – some answers

- Here are some answers you might give to a すき ですか question:

    はい、大すき です。 *hai, daisuki desu.*
    Yes, I love it.

    はい、すき です。 *hai, suki desu.*
    Yes, I like it.

    まあまあ すき です。 *maamaa suki desu.*
    It's OK.

    いいえ、あまり … (すきじゃない です。) *iie, amari … (suki janai desu.)*
    No, not much.

    いいえ、すきじゃない です。 *iie, suki janai desu.*
    No, I don't (like it).

- So far you have been reading 大 as おお in 大きい but here you read it as だい *dai*. As you know 大 means 'big' so when you use it with すき *suki* you're saying you like it 'big time'.
- The negative form of すき です (like) is すきじゃない です (don't like).
- When you answer あまり … to a すき ですか question, people understand that you're using a shorthand way of saying あまり すきじゃない です, which means 'I don't like it very much'.

17

だい二か
十七

だい二か

Likes and dislikes – some statements

わたしは まんがが すき です。

▶ To say (without anyone asking) that you like something say
わたしは (thing) が すき です。
watashi wa (thing) ga suki desu.

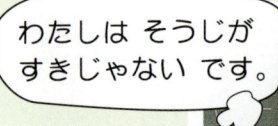

わたしは そうじが すきじゃない です。

▶ To say that you don't like something say
わたしは (thing) が すきじゃない です。
watashi wa (thing) ga suki janai desu.

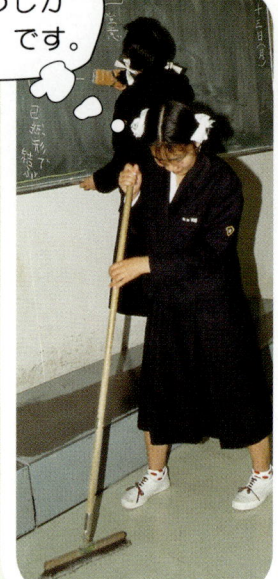

▶ To state that someone else likes something say
(person) は (thing) が すき です。
(person) wa (thing) ga suki desu.

まさるさんは しゅくだいが 大すき です。

しましょう

Wheel balancing

Draw up a wheel like the one you see here and write in the section headings. Now 'balance' the wheel by choosing one word from the たんご on page 16 to write in each segment.

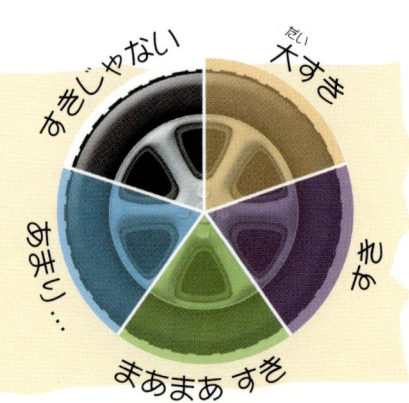

すきじゃない / 大すき / きらい / まあまあ すき / あまい…

十八

口 れんしゅう

The animal popularity chart

Help conduct a survey to find out which are the most popular animals in your class. In your *Workbook* you will find a survey sheet, which you will use to record your results. Here's what to do:

- Select a classmate to interview and fill in their name and age at the top of the survey sheet.

- Interview your classmate and ask whether they like the animals pictured. (The Japanese words for these animals are listed too, but don't expect them to be in the same order.)

- As you ask about each animal your partner will tell you whether they love it, like it, think it's OK, not like it very much or not like it at all.

- As your classmate answers your question about each animal, place a tick in the appropriate column on the survey sheet.

- In the てん (points) column write a score for each animal:

大すき：	5
すき：	4
まあまあ すき：	3
あまり すきじゃない：	2
すきじゃない：	1

- Now use your results to contribute to the overall scores on the class survey sheet. Your class can then publish its animal popularity chart.

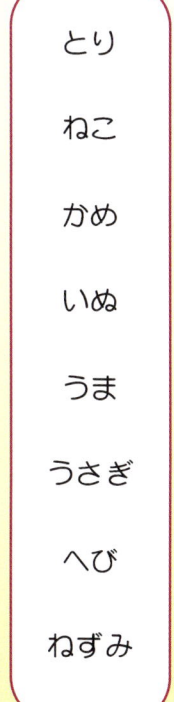

うさぎが すき ですか。

いいえ、あまり すき じゃない です。

うさぎは ２てん

とり
ねこ
かめ
いぬ
うま
うさぎ
へび
ねずみ

だい二か

十九

口 れんしゅう

Warm-up

- These are the Japanese words you need to go with the pictures. Make sure your partner can read them all correctly.

    cho ko re e to
    チョコレート   すいえい   にく   そうじ

    ke e ki   *jo gi n gu*
    ケーキ   れんしゅう   ジョギング   かいもの

    ぎゅうにゅう   しゅくだい

- Make sure your partner knows which word goes with which picture by having them point to the correct picture as you say **five** of the words. Now swap roles.

- Point to **five** of the pictures and your partner will say the words. Now swap roles.

だい二か

Talking seriously

- Ask your partner if they like **five** of the things in the pictures. For example, you could ask
ジョギングが すき ですか。
<small>jo gi n gu</small>

- As you ask about each thing, your partner will tell you whether they love it, like it, think it's OK, not like it very much, or not like it at all.

- Your partner will ask you about the other **five** things.

れんしゅう

だい二か

えみ

ひろし

ちひろ

二十二

しん

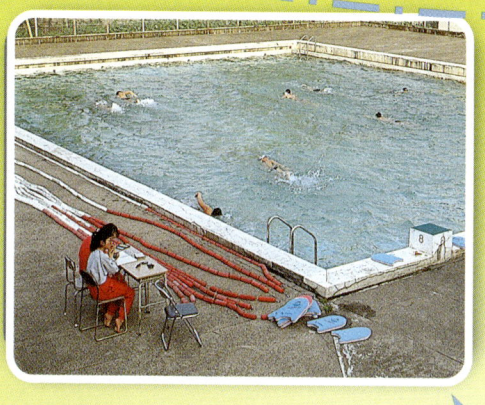

Do you like it?
Without waiting to be asked, tell your partner how you feel about each thing you see pictured here. Do you love it, like it, not like it much, or not like it at all? Listen attentively to your partner's feelings about the same things.

What about them?

1. Enough about you – what about the people on these pages? Follow the lines that connect them with the different things around them, work out how they feel and then make an appropriate statement.

   •••••••••• means they love it;
   ────── means they like it;
   ─ ─ ─ means they don't like it very much;
   ━ ━ ━ means they just don't like it.

   For example, if you follow the ─ ─ ─ from しん you will want to say:
   しんさんは すいえいが あまり すきじゃない です。

2. Now get your partner involved again and see if they can follow the lines. You could ask, for example: えみさんは にくが すき ですか。

   You would expect them to answer: いいえ、あまり すきじゃない です。

だい二か

二十三

かんじ

Here are some new かんじ for you to practise.

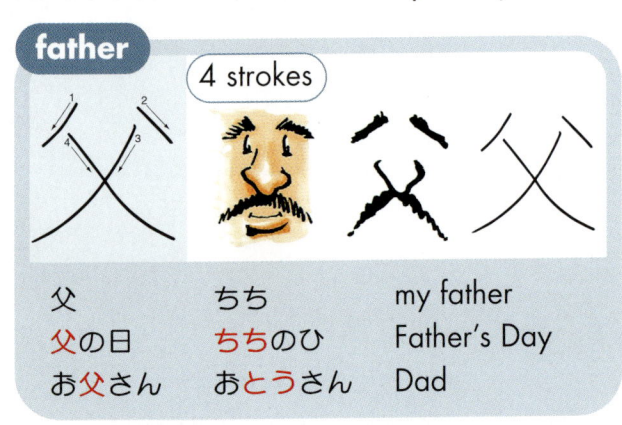

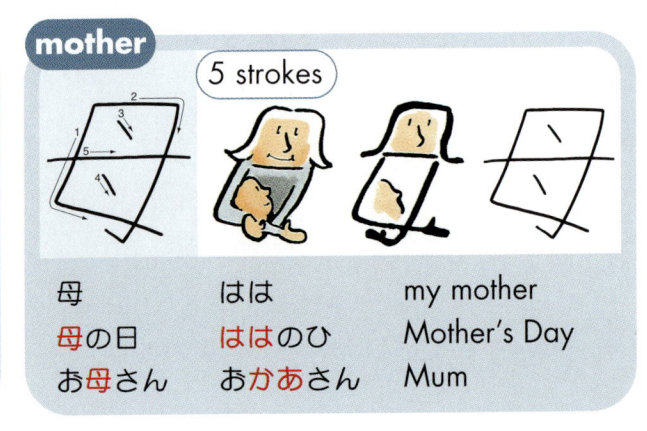

father — 4 strokes

父	ちち	my father
父の日	ちちのひ	Father's Day
お父さん	おとうさん	Dad

mother — 5 strokes

母	はは	my mother
母の日	ははのひ	Mother's Day
お母さん	おかあさん	Mum

Here are two new かんじ readings.

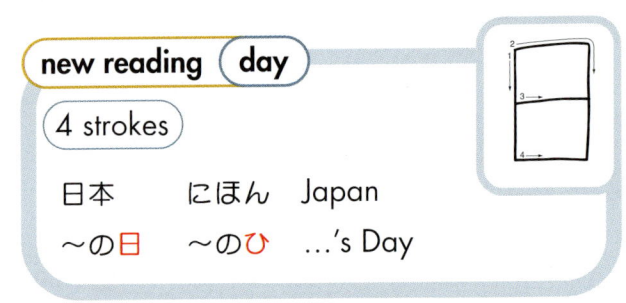

new reading — big — 3 strokes

大きい	おおきい	big
大すき	だいすき	like a lot, love

new reading — day — 4 strokes

日本	にほん	Japan
～の日	～のひ	…'s Day

母の日、父の日、こどもの日

Japanese sons and daughters have the same sort of opportunities to celebrate their parents as you have; the second Sunday in May is set aside for 母の日, and Dad can look forward to 父の日 on the third Sunday in June.

These parents' days are simply chances for children to say 'thank you', so the wording on cards that children give their parents is usually pretty straightforward.

Shops all over Japan get into the spirit of these days and have special displays and catalogues offering all sorts of treats for Mum and Dad. Food stores, in particular, package all sorts of delicacies to guarantee a tasty family celebration. They may not go for the special meat, noodle or sushi packs, but many dutiful sons and daughters line up for that special 母の日 or 父の日 cake. The day just wouldn't be the same without it!

Japan has another special celebration that the rest of the world needs to catch up with – こどもの日, Children's Day.

It's on May 5, and it's not just a private family celebration, it's a national holiday!

One traditional sign of こどもの日 is carp streamers flying over houses where there are boy children. When the wind catches them they look just like those brave fish that swim upstream against strong currents, even up waterfalls, to reach their breeding ground. These streamers, called こいのぼり (climbing carp) remind boys that they need strength and determination to succeed in life.

Another sign that May 5 has come around is the appearance of dolls dressed in samurai warrior armour. These dolls reinforce the idea that life is a battle. Surrounded by samurai weapons, the warrior dolls make an impressive display, but there is no way Japanese boys would be allowed to treat them as action figures and play with them. They are far too expensive for that!

If こどもの日 sounds a bit boyish, that's because May 5 used to be called Boys' Day. Girls still have Girls' Day on March 3, which also happens to be Dolls' Day. But girls are full partners in こどもの日. It's just that they don't usually bother with こいのぼり and warrior dolls – they don't need special reminders that we all need to be determined.

All the shops get in on the act on こどもの日, with foreign outlets anxious to show that they have embraced Japanese culture. As on the other family days there is a wide array of traditional and modern mouth-watering treats available. But something nearly everyone goes for is – you guessed it – cake!

しましょう

Express your gratitude to a parent and show off your Japanese skills at the same time by designing a Father's or Mother's Day card. And while you're at it, why not design a card that your parents can give you on Children's Day? They deserve a chance to tell you what a great kid you are.

Bath time

Here's the situation: you're on a home-stay in Japan, you've had dinner with your host family (although お父さん still hasn't come home from work yet) when お母さん points towards the bathroom and says to you, おふろ、どうぞ. Not only is your host mother announcing that it's bath time, she's offering you the privilege of first bath.

You get your stuff from your bedroom, go to the bathroom door, take off your slippers and go in. You see the おふろ as soon as you enter the bathroom: it is a deep tub full of the steaming hot water that お母さん has already run for the family. But don't go there … yet.

In another part of the room you see a couple of taps or a hand-held shower, a stool and a plastic basin. Go *there*, for this is where you actually clean yourself up. All the soaping, scrubbing and shampooing happens here, with you seated on a stool.

Now that you're squeaky clean, having rinsed off every bit of soap and shampoo, hop into the bath for a relaxing soak. As you lower yourself in you'll notice that the water is very hot, but whatever you do, don't add any cold water. This water has to stay crystal clear and piping hot for the whole family. That's right, everyone from お父さん to おとうとさん has to use the same water you are now soaking in. So it might even pay to put your hair up if it is threatening to float on the surface of the bath water.

See how it works? The おふろ is not for cleaning, but for soaking and relaxing. And the water is to be shared with all members of the family. So resist the urge to pull out the plug and watch the water go down the drain!

べんきょうページ

Family talk

(Picture 1) おにいさん、しずかに して！

(Picture 2) お母さん、おにいさんは うるさい です。

(Picture 3) ゆきお！ はやく！
おとうとさんは おもしろい ですね。

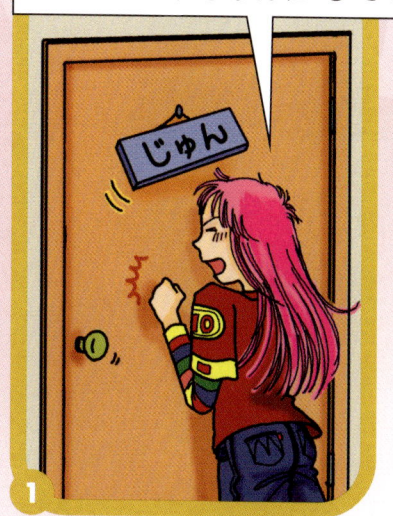

Family talk

▶ Here are some new 'family' words that you need:
- when you are speaking to your parents or to your brothers and sisters;
- when you are talking about your parents, brothers or sisters to someone else in your family;
- when you are talking about someone else's parents, brothers or sisters.

たんご

お父さん	Dad	your father	父	my father
お母さん	Mum	your mother	母	my mother
おにいさん	'big brother'	your big brother	あに	my big brother
おねえさん	'big sister'	your big sister	あね	my big sister
おとうとさん	*	your little brother	おとうと	my little brother
いもうとさん	*	your little sister	いもうと	my little sister

- Notice how きょうこ, in picture 3 above, addressed ゆきお? She's right, of course. When you are talking to your little brother or sister you simply use their name, without さん.
- When you are talking to someone else about their little brother or sister you can use their name (plus さん) if you know it. So りつこ could have used ゆきお's name instead of referring to him as おとうとさん. Either way is fine.

だい二か

27　二十七

🗣 れんしゅう

Here is a page from your family album showing your dad and mum, and your brothers and sisters.

すごい

大きい

小さい

うるさい

かわいい

きたない

Warm-up

- Your partner points to a family member and you say who it is. For example, if your partner points to your father, you say 父.

- You point to a family member and your partner says who it is. For example, you point to your father, and your partner says お父さん.

- Your partner points to a family member and you choose a suitable adjective to describe them. Your partner points to your father, you say 大きい.

Talking seriously

Point to the various members of your family and say who they are. For example, point to your father and say 父 です.

- Your partner looks at the person you're pointing to and makes a comment about them, using the adjectives given. In this case they would say: お父さんは 大きい ですね.

Here is the next page from your family album, with photos showing your parents, brothers and sisters doing things they're really into.

たんご
します
よみます
見ます
ききます

Warm-up
- Point to the various members of your family and say who they are. Your partner says who they are from their point of view. You say 父 です, your partner says お父さん です.
- Your partner names a family member and you say what they are doing. Your partner says お父さん, you say まんがを よみます.

Talking seriously
- Your partner points to the various members of your family and asks whether they often do what they are doing in the photo. You reply yes, they really like it.

For example:

- ◼ お父さんは よく まんがを よみますか。
- ● はい、父は まんがが 大すき です。

しましょう

1. Practise with your family. What are you going to call your mum and dad, big brother or big sister? If your little brother or sister feels left out, give them a Japanese name.

2. Remember たんご tennis that you played on page 5? Try it again here with the new family words. You serve 父 and your classmate returns with お父さん …

3. Sing the family song へえ！おもしろい！ It's on the *Hai! 3* Audio CDs and you have the words in your *Workbook*.

だい二か

二十九

父の日

だい二か

1. 山口(やまぐち)さんの うちで。父の日 です。
お父さんは ゴルフ(go ru fu)に 行きます。

　いってきます！　　いってらっしゃい！

2. （そうじ）

3. わたしは そうじが すきじゃない です。

4. お母さん、わたしと りつこさんとゆきおは かいものに 行きます。お母さんは？
　わたしは 父の日の りょうりを します。

5. えっ！ほんとう？りょうりを しますか。

6. まちの デパート(de pa a to)で。
父の日のギフト
すき ですか。

7. いいえ、あまり…
いいえ、すき じゃない です。

8. すき ですか。なまえは Racy です。
はい、すき です。

9. ありがとう ございます。

10. おねえさん、見て！父の日の テイクアウト(te i ku a u to) です。いい プレゼント(pu re ze n to) です。
父の日のメニュー

11. でも、お母さんは 父の日の りょうりを します。
えっ！ほんとう？

三十　　　　　　　　　　　　　　　　　　　30

12 山口さんの うちで。

わたしは りょうりが すきじゃない です。

13 ああ、おもしろい！大すき です。

14 デパートで。 見て！ゴルフ。

15 お父さんは ゴルフが すき ですか。 はい、大すき です。

16

17 見て...『お父さん、ありがとう！』いい ですね。

18 そう ですね。ぼくは この ゴルフボールを かいます。

19 いい プレゼント です。

20

21 おねえさん、見て。おにいさん です。

22 おにいさん、ともだちの りつこさん です。

23 りつこ です。こんにちは。 きょうこの あに です。じゅん です。こんにちは。

24 何 ですか。

25

26 父の日の すし です。ぼくは この すしを かいます。

27 おにいさん、お母さんは 父の日の りょうりを します。 えっ！ほんとう？

だい二か

たんご			
(place)で	at (a place)	この	this
りょうり	cooking, cuisine	カード	card
えっ？ほんとう？	Oh, really?!	けち	stingy, tight
でも	but	どうしよう？！	What will I do?!

1. What day is it? How is きょうこ's dad going to spend it?
2. What are きょうこ and ゆきお planning to do? What about Mum?
3. Why does ゆきお want to buy the special takeaway? Why doesn't he get it?
4. How does Mum feel about doing the cooking?
5. What does じゅん want to buy for his dad? Why doesn't he get it?
6. What is Mum's problem? How does she solve it?

Time out!

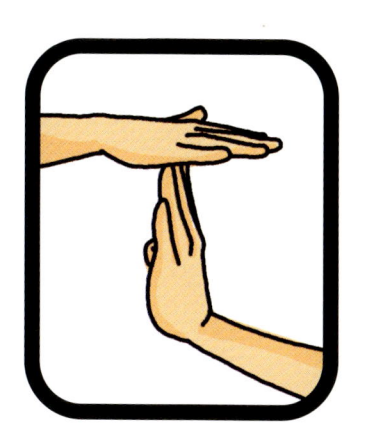

だい3か

When we call **'Time out!'** we are signalling it's time for a break. You have been working hard on your Japanese language, so we think it's time to slow things down a bit so you can get some energy back before we push on.

In **Time out!**, however, we won't be stopping the clock; in fact we will start it running as you learn:

- to tell the time when it's 5, 15, 25 (etc.) minutes past the hour
- to tell the time when it's 10, 20, 30 (etc.) minutes past the hour
- to read and write the kanji 時, 分 and 半.

In this chapter you will also come of age as a Japanese reader as you 'trash' roomaji.

べんきょうページ (pee ji)

It's five past

5 ふん **go**fun

55 ふん gojuu**go**fun
or
5 ふんまえ **go**fun mae

15 ふん juu**go**fun

45 ふん yonjuu**go**fun

25 ふん nijuu**go**fun

35 ふん sanjuu**go**fun

いま、何じ ですか。
1じ 15ふん です。

It's ten past

10 ぷん **jup**pun

50 ぷん **go**juppun
or
10 ぷんまえ **jup**pun mae

20 ぷん ni**jup**pun

40 ぷん yon**jup**pun

30 ぷん san**jup**pun
or はん

いま、何じ ですか。
7じ 20ぷん です。

三十三

かんじ

Here are some new かんじ for you to practise.

minute — 4 strokes

| 5分 | ごふん | 5 minutes |
| 10分 | じゅっぷん | 10 minutes |

o'clock, hour — 10 strokes

1時	いちじ	one o'clock
9時20分	くじにじゅっぷん	9:20
何時	なんじ	what time?

half — 5 strokes

| 4時半 | よじはん | 4:30 |

しましょう

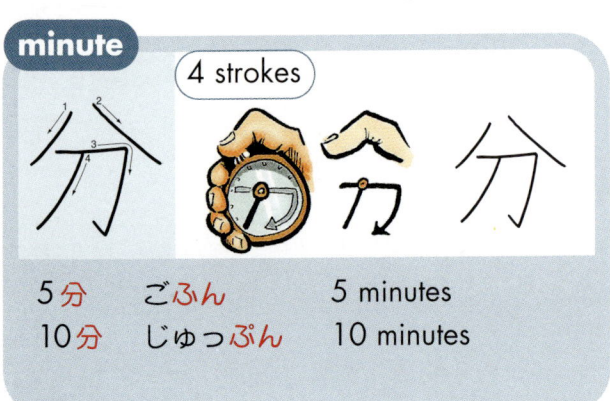

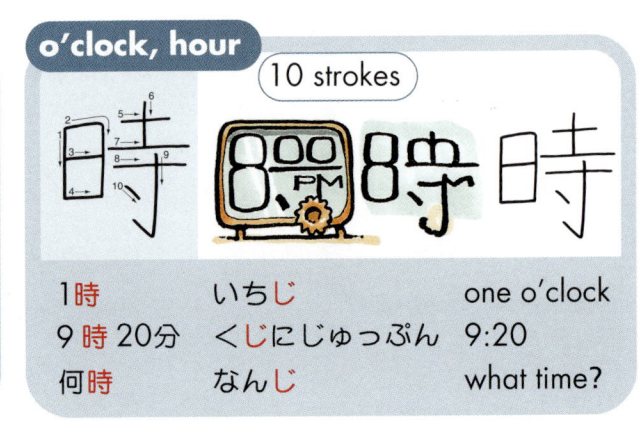

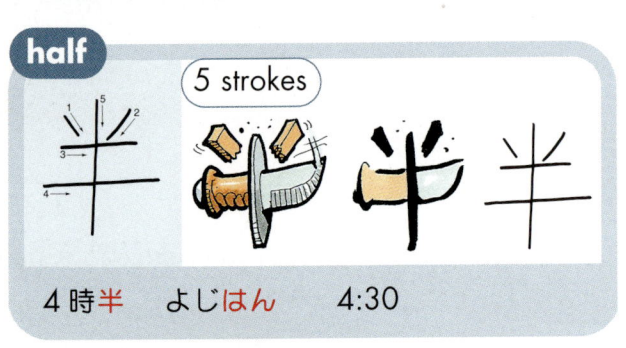

Where will you park?

These two car parks, **A** and **B**, are near each other in Tokyo. One of them is open around the clock, the other closes overnight. The one that stays open has special night rates. (夜間 やかん means 'during the night'.) Prices are, of course, in 円 yen.

- I parked in **A** from 11 am until 1 pm. How much would I have saved if I'd parked in **B**?

- I parked in **A** from 10 pm until 11 pm. How much would I have saved if I'd parked in **B**?

- I'm a slow learner. I parked in **A** again and went to a movie that finished at midnight. What problem did I face when I went to pick up my car?

A: IN P 満車 7時-23時30分 30分 300円 新宿センタービル

B: TOKYO PUBLIC 100円 20分 夜 100円/60分 間 (PM10:00〜AM8:00)

It's five past

▸ To tell the time at 5 past the hour, you simply add 5分 *gofun* to the 時 *ji* time.

For example, when it's 5 past six (6:05 on your digital clock) you say 6時 5分 です。 *rokuji gofun desu*.

Now it's easy to go around the clock and tell the time at every '5 past' time: 15, 25, 35, 45, 55 分.

3時 25分 です。

It's ten past

▸ To tell the time at 10 past the hour, you simply add 10分 *juppun* to the 時 *ji* time.

For example, when it's 10 past six (6:10 on your digital clock) you say 6時 10分 です。 *rokuji juppun desu*.

Now it's easy to go around the clock and tell the time at every '10 past' time: 20, 30, 40, 50 分.

▸ Remember that Japanese has a 'half' when it comes to time.

6時 半 です。 It's half past six.

9時 20分 です。

Is it 'past' or 'to'?

▸ Once the clock ticks past the half-hour mark, you can read it as 'past' the hour it has left or 'to' the hour it is approaching.

2時 50分 です。 It's 2:50.

or

3時 10分 まえ です。 It's 10 to three.

▸ まえ means 'before' or 'in front of'. It is mainly used with '10 to' and '5 to' times.

2時 50分 です。
3時 10分 まえ です。

たんご

〜時	... o'clock	5分　ごふん	5 minutes
〜時半	half past ...	10分　じゅっぷん	10 minutes
〜分、〜分	... minutes	まえ	before, in front of

だい三か

れんしゅう

Warm-up

Look at the times pictured on this page and choose one to say in 日本語. Your partner will point to the clock or watch showing that time. Then they will say a time for you to point to.

The aim is to be able to tell the time on all the clocks and watches, so help each other if you get stuck. がんばって！

だい三か

三十六

Talking seriously

With your partner, decide who will be talking about the clocks numbered 1–6 and who will be specialising in 7–12.

Now point to a clock or watch in your partner's territory and politely ask what time it is. Don't forget to say thanks when you get your answer. Then your partner will point to a clock or a watch and ask you the time. If you need to buy some thinking time before you answer, throw in some Japanese 'ums' and 'ahs'.

Let's trash roomaji!

We know you have been feeling restless about roomaji. Why, you ask, are you still reading Japanese with roomaji tacked on to the ひらがな and かんじ? After all, you don't still ride around with training wheels fixed to your bike.

It's time to become a fully-fledged Japanese reader now, time to enjoy the privilege of reading ひらがな and かんじ without roomaji getting in the way. This is a real coming of age: it means more independence, it means getting there under your own steam.

Reading with roomaji

Reading without roomaji

What an important moment this is! What a cause for celebration! You are now ready for your 'さようなら roomaji' party in which the main event is the ceremonial dumping of roomaji into a rubbish bin.

Your teacher will be planning a final ひらがな test before the party, so take this last chance to really learn every corner of the ひらがな chart. がんばれ！

このじは、何ですか。

The じ of かんじ (and the ji of roomaji) means 'letter' or 'symbol', and この means 'this'. So if an occasional ひらがな or かんじ slips your mind, you can always ask: 先生、このじは、何ですか。

Never be afraid to ask. Learning to read Japanese is a long journey and Japanese students are always learning new characters and revising old ones.

At least, with roomaji in the trash, you can make the journey without those training wheels.

しましょう

Sign here

Now that you are a real ひらがな reader, here are some Japanese signs for you to try your skills on. They are all names of places around town. Notice how sign-writers always go for attractive, interesting-looking lettering.

Point to four of the signs, say よんで, and your trusty partner will read what it says. They will then test you on the other four.

1. みずま
2. おかじや
3. なかがき
4. ふるさと
5. さんのまち
6. それから
7. あけぼの
8. たぬき

だい三か

三十九

39

だい 4 か

What a day!

べんきょうページ

I get up at …

わたしは 7時に おきます。

And then I have breakfast

そして、あさごはんを たべます。

Dad goes to work at …

父は 7時半に しごとに 行きます。

And I go to school at …

そして、わたしは 7時 45分に がっこうに 行きます。

ゆきお、はやく。

In だい4か you will learn:

- to talk about your daily routine, including getting up, going to bed, going to school, getting home, and having breakfast, snacks and dinner
- to ask someone else what time they do something
- to ask someone else what they do, eat, drink, and so on
- to read and write the kanji 校 and 食
- a new way of reading 何
- about breakfast in Japan
- about using chopsticks

だい四か

四十

40

I get home at …

5
- 4時半に うちに かえります。
- お母さん、ただいま。
- おかえりなさい。

And then I have a snack

6
- そして、おやつを たべます。
- おいしい ですね。
- そう ですね。

Dad gets home at …

7
- 父は 7時に うちに かえります。
- ただいま！ばんごはん です。

And then we have dinner

8
- そして、ばんごはんを たべます。
- いただきます。ああ、おいしい です。

I go to bed at …

9
- わたしは 10時半に ねます。
- おやすみなさい。

Talking about your daily routine

▶ To talk about your daily routine, you say you do something **at** a particular time. To do this in Japanese you put particle に after the time.

わたしは 7時に おきます。
I get up at 7 o'clock.

7時 45 分に がっこうに 行きます。
I go to school at 7:45.

Asking and answering about daily routine

▶ To find out about someone else's routine you ask what time they do something **at**. To do this in Japanese you put particle に after 何時. Here are some sample questions and answers:

何時に おきますか。
(At) what time do you get up?

8時に おきます。
I get up at 8 o'clock.

何時に がっこうに 行きますか。
(At) what time do you go to school?

8時半に 行きます。
I go at 8:30.

▶ You use particle に to make clear what time someone does something **at**, and what place someone is going **to**. に comes right after the time or the place.

父は 8時に しごとに 行きます。
My dad goes to work at 8 o'clock.

5時半に うちに かえります。
I get home at 5:30.

(time) に	at (a time)	しごと	work
そして	And, And then	がっこう	school
		おやつ	snack
おきます	get up	おいしい	yummy
かえります	go home	あさごはん	breakfast
たべます	eat	ばんごはん	dinner
ねます	go to bed		
		こんばんは	Good evening
		おやすみ なさい	Good night

かんじ

Here are some new かんじ for you to practise.

eat — 9 strokes

食

| 食べます | たべます | eat |
| 食べません | たべません | don't eat |

- The kanji 食 is only the た part of 食べます, so remember to add the rest after the かんじ.

place of learning — 10 strokes

校

| 学校 | がっこう | school |

- 学 *gaku* has been shortened to *gak* in the word for 'school' as it is easier to say *gakkou* than *gakukou*.

new reading — what?

何 — 7 strokes

何人	なんにん	how many people?
何さい	なんさい	how old?
何時	なんじ	what time?
何	なに	what?

しましょう

Night owl, early bird

Put this question to people in your group: 何時に ねますか。

Who goes to bed the latest? Compare your group's time with other groups' times to discover the class **night owl**.

Now think of a question you can ask to find the class **early bird**. Answers to this question will also uncover your class's *latest* riser. This person wins the title of あさねぼう (sleepy head).

Last one home is …

Form a line according to the time you get home from school. To find your place in the line, ask classmates what time they get home and work out whether you are earlier or later. Who gets home the earliest? How do they manage that? Who is last home? What's happening there?

何時に うちに かえりますか。

4時に かえります。

だい四か

ロ れんしゅう

Warm-up

- Point to a picture and your partner will tell you the person's name and what time they get home from school.

- Your partner will point to a picture and you say what the person does when they get home. You get to choose from this list:

    しゅくだいを します。

    おやつを 食べます。

    おんがくを ききます。

    ばんごはんを 食べます。

    テレビを 見ます。
    _{te re bi}

Talking seriously

- Look at what these people do when they get home from school.

- Choose a person and tell your partner about their routine. For example, if you talk about たかさん you could say:

    たかさんは 4時に うちに かえります。

    そして、おやつを 食べます。

だい四か

四十四

44

口 れんしゅう

けん

本田(だ)さん

Live and let live

In Japan rock stars and rice farmers follow different daily routines. Find out more about this by asking the people pictured here what time they get up, go to work, get home and go to bed. These are the questions you can ask:

- 何時に おきますか。
- 何時に しごとに 行きますか。
- 何時に うちに かえりますか。
- 何時に ねますか。

Your partner will answer for them.

This is about you

Your daily routine is as important as anyone else's, so tell your partner all about it. You get up at …

だい四か

いただきます！

When you go to Japan you might take a while to get used to breakfast time. If you're there as a tourist you'll soon find a Western-style fast-food place to serve you a breakfast to remind you of home. But if you're lucky enough to have a home-stay and to experience Japanese family life, you'll probably be offered a traditional Japanese breakfast.

You will notice that the word for 'rice' is ごはん, and that the word for 'breakfast' is あさごはん – literally 'morning rice'. Over the years ごはん took on a broader meaning, especially in words like あさごはん and ばんごはん. But the word still reminds us of the importance of rice in Japanese meals, breakfast included.

A traditional Japanese breakfast can consist of rice, fish or egg, pickles, nori (seaweed) and miso soup. Miso, served with many meals, is a delicious soybean soup. You may not be used to eating anything quite so nourishing for breakfast, so it may take a while to develop a taste for it.

Many Japanese families have both types of breakfast available and family members will eat what they feel like. You can do that too – but don't forget to say いただきます before you start. You're not wishing other people at the table an enjoyable meal; you're saying something like 'I humbly receive'. You might even join your hands as you say it, as you'll sometimes see Japanese people do.

There's another thing to get used to at meal times in Japan: おはし, chopsticks. Using chopsticks is a skill everyone in Japan has to learn, Japanese people included. Japanese children often get to practise with chopsticks that are stuck together at the top. This gives the 'apprentice' chopstick user a feel for how they operate. Other learners start with chopsticks that have grooves towards the bottom so that food doesn't slip off.

いただきます。

だい四か

四十六

おはし come in many different styles, from deluxe ornamental ones for special occasions, to cheap wooden ones that you have to separate yourself. Watch out for these: many a meal has been spoilt by a splinter in the tongue, so rub them smooth before you start eating. Maybe you could follow the example of some people in Japan who avoid the cheap disposable sticks and carry a pair that really suit them wherever they go. Not only do they avoid splinters – think how many trees they are saving!

When you do use おはし there are a few 'do's' and 'don'ts' to keep in mind. If you are reaching for a piece of food try to be accurate: if possible, take from the edge of the dish and don't touch other food. When you have finished with them, place your おはし across your bowl or on the はしおき (chopstick rests) that you may find in front of it.

If you do these things you will get a reputation for Very Good Manners. On the other hand, try to avoid the old trap of using one of your おはし to spear your food.

And don't use your おはし to go rummaging around in a dish, looking for the good bits! Nor should you hover over a dish, waving your おはし around while you decide what to have next. Avoid passing food to others with your おはし, and don't leave your sticks standing up in your food.

All of these practices come under the heading of Very Bad Manners. But you're no Maggie McGaffe, so have a go with your おはし and enjoy your meal. And if the person who prepared it is within earshot, show your appreciation by saying ごちそうさま, 'thanks for the food'.

どうぞ。

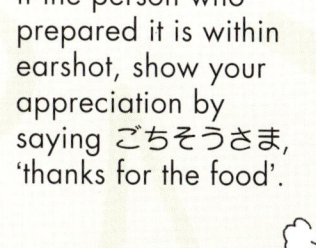

いただきます。

だい四か

47

べんきょうページ

What do you have for breakfast?

こんにちは！

まさる です。

ぼくは あさごはんに、さかなと ごはんを 食べます。

みそしるを のみます。

そして、ジュースを のみます。

みなさん、あさごはんに 何を 食べますか。

何を のみますか。

おはよう ございます。

わたしは ゆうか です。

あさごはんに、シリアルを 食べます。コーンフレークが 大すき です。

そして、ぎゅうにゅうを のみます。

みなさん、あさごはんに 何を 食べますか。

何を のみますか。

だい四か

四十八

48

Asking what people do

▶ When you ask what people do, eat, drink and so on, you put particle を after 何. In these questions you read 何 as なに.

> しゅうまつに 何を しますか。
> What do you do on the weekend?

> あさごはんに 何を 食べますか。
> What do you have for breakfast?

▶ Notice the use of particle に in the sentences above to say *on* the weekend and *for* breakfast. In English we could also say *at* the weekend, *at* breakfast time.

And, another thing ...

▶ Use と to link two nouns (things, animals or people).

> あさごはんに さかなと ごはんを 食べます。
> I eat fish and rice for breakfast.

▶ Use そして to link two activities, one coming after the other. In Japanese そして always starts a new sentence.

> わたしは しゅくだいを します。そして、１０時半に ねます。
> I do my homework and then I go to bed at half past ten.

> みそしるを のみます。そして、ジュース を のみます。
> I have some miso soup and then I drink some juice.

(In English, when it comes to food and drink you often say 'have' rather than 'eat' or 'drink'. In Japanese you always say 食べます and のみます.)

たんご

Breakfast

あさごはん	breakfast
あさごはんに	for breakfast, at breakfast time
食べます	eat
のみます	drink

Things to eat

さかな	fish
ごはん	cooked rice, meal
シリアル	cereal
トースト	toast

Things to drink

ジュース	juice
コーヒー	coffee
こうちゃ	tea
おちゃ	green tea
みそしる	miso (soybean) soup

だい四か

ロれんしゅう

だい四か

おさむ　　　　しずか

Warm-up

1 As you read these 'food and drink' words your partner will point to the pictures of them.

| おちゃ | こうちゃ | コーヒー（*ko o hi i*） | シリアル（*shi ri a ru*） | みそしる |
| ごはん | さかな | ジュース（*ju u su*） | トースト（*to o su to*） | |

2 What colour is the 食べます line? What about the のみます line?

五十

こうすけ　　　　　　　　　ともこ

Talking seriously

In とうきょう, the Asahi News is running a survey to find out which sort of breakfast is more popular in Japan: the traditional breakfast of fish, rice and miso soup (わしょく) or the Western-style breakfast with cereal and toast (ようしょく).

As one of their roving reporters, your job is to interview the people (played by your partner) on this page and the opposite page about their breakfast eating and drinking habits. Here is how one interview might go:

You:	すみません、おなまえは？
Partner:	(Name)です。
You:	(Name)さん、あさごはんに 何を 食べますか。
Partner:	(Food)を 食べます。
You:	わしょく ですね。OR ようしょく ですね。
Partner:	そう ですね。
You:	そして、何を のみますか。
Partner:	(Drink)を のみます。
You:	ありがとう ございます。

だい四か

五十一

51

よみれんしゅう

山口さんの かぞくは よく テイクアウトを かいますね。ばんごはんに KFCの チキンを 食べます。大すき です。
この テイクアウトを 見て ください。

ファミリーセット
4〜5人前　3,200円

ファミリーパック
4人前　¥2460

ファミリーも満足4〜5人前
超グッド 36cm
¥500引 ¥2,000
8カット

Now answer these questions.

1. How many people will each takeaway item feed?
2. How much does each cost in your currency?
3. Which do you think is the best value for the Yamaguchi family? (Remember: かぞくは 五人 です。)
4. If you were home-staying with the Yamaguchis, how would you tell them which of these takeaway foods you like?

じゃんけん！

1. 7時 です。山口（やまぐち）さんの かぞくは ばんごはんを 食べます。
   いただきます！

2. わたしは えびが 大すき です。

3. （皿の絵）

4. （顔）

5. だれの えび ですか。

6. わたしの えび です。
   ぼくの です。
   じゃ、じゃんけん…

7. （お母さん）

8. じゃん、けん、ぽん！

9. あ〜あ！

10. ああ、おいしい！

11. ごちそうさま！

12. 7時半 です。

13. お母さん、いま テレビ（terebi）を 見ますか。
    いいえ、見ません。

だい四か

五十三

だい四か

14. 「POP 10」を 見ましょう。

15. いいえ、「ビッグ・ブラザー」を 見ましょう！

16. ぼくは 「にんじゃ 大一」が すき です。

17. お母さん！

18. じゃ、じゃんけん...

19. じゃん けん ぽん！

20. 「ビッグ・ブラザー」は 日本語で 「おにいさん」 ですね。 はい。

21. わたしは ビッグ・ブラザー が すきじゃない です。

22. 日曜日 です。

23. きょう、わたしは かいものに 行きます。みなさん、何を しますか。
わたしと ゆきおは すいえいに 行きます。

24. 10時半に ゴルフに 行きます。

25. ぼくは ともだちの うちに 行きます。そして、バンドの れんしゅうを します。

26. うちは きたない です。そうじは？

27. そうじ？

28. じゃ、じゃんけん...

29. !!

30. いってきます。 / いってらっしゃい。

31. わたしは じゃんけんが すきじゃない です！

32. 5時です。 ただいま！

33. おかえりなさい。

34. きょうこ、見て。えびチップス です。

35. うわあ！

36. ビッグ・ブラザー が すきですか。 / はい、はい。大すきです。

37. じゃ、どうぞ。 / ありがとう！

だい四か

五十五

55

だい四か

38 ばんごはんに すしを 食べます。

- おいしい ですね。
- そう ですね。
- **39** すしが 大すき です。
- **40**
- **41**
- だれの ですか。
- わたしの です。
- ぼくの です。
- じゃ…
- えっ、じゃんけん！
- **42** **43** **44** **45** **46**
- じゃん、けん…
- ぽん！
- どうぞ！
- お母さん、ありがとう！
- いただきます。
- **47** **48** **49** **50**

たんご

えび	prawn	じゃんけん	paper, rock, scissors game	日本語で	in Japanese
じゃ	OK then			日曜日	Sunday
		見ましょう	let's watch	きょう	today

1. There is a problem at the dinner table. What is it, and how does Mum solve it?
2. What do you notice about the way きょうこ plays じゃんけん?
3. Who wants to watch a 'reality' TV show? What is it called?
4. What is きょうこ planning to do today? What about the others?
5. What problem is solved by this round of じゃんけん?
6. How does きょうこ feel about じゃんけん? Why?
7. How does じゅん tease きょうこ when he gets home?
8. Why does きょうこ look so worried near the end of the story? What cheers her up?

Happy days!

だい 5 か

Well done! You've worked very hard and you've made it to the last section of this book. We are celebrating this by easing off on the amount of new language and giving you a chance to put together everything you have done so far. Happy days!

As far as new material goes, you will learn:

- to ask and tell what day of the week it is
- to say what day something is on
- to read and write the kanji 月, 火, 水, 木, 金, 土 and 曜
- a new way to read 日
- about a famous Japanese tourist trail
- to sing about the days of the week

べんきょうページ (pe e ji)

What day is it today?

ゆきお、7時半 です。

きょうは 何曜日 ですか。

水曜日 です。はやく！

What day is it on?

バンド(ba n do)の れんしゅうは 何曜日 ですか。

バンド(ba n do)の れんしゅうは 木曜日 です。

たんご

きょう			today
何曜日	なんようび		what day?
日曜日	にちようび	(Sun-day)	Sunday
月曜日	げつようび	(Moon-day)	Monday
火曜日	かようび	(Fire-day)	Tuesday
水曜日	すいようび	(Water-day)	Wednesday
木曜日	もくようび	(Wood-day)	Thursday
金曜日	きんようび	(Metal-day)	Friday
土曜日	どようび	(Earth-day)	Saturday

Japanese days of the week take their names from seven basic elements of nature. We have a Sun-day and Moon-day in English too, but the days of the rest of the week are named after ancient gods. Thursday, for example, is named after Thor, the god of thunder.

だい五か

五十七

かんじ

Here are some new かんじ and a new reading.

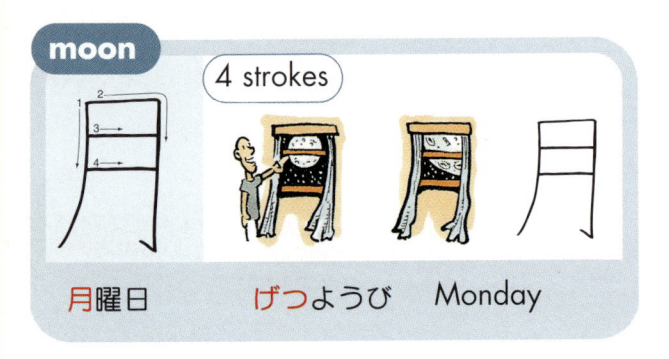

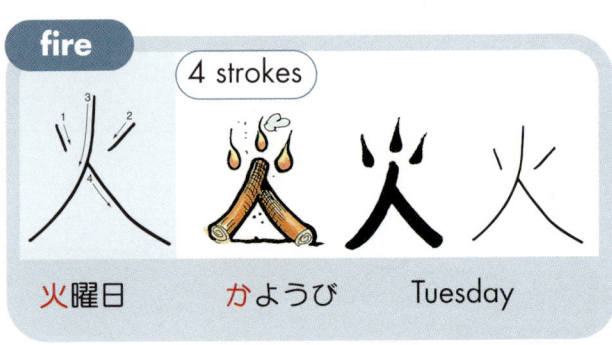

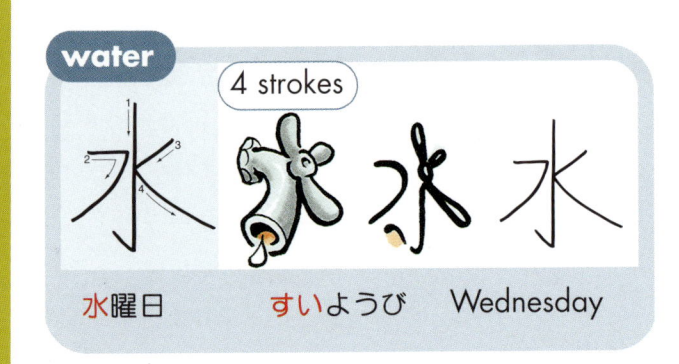

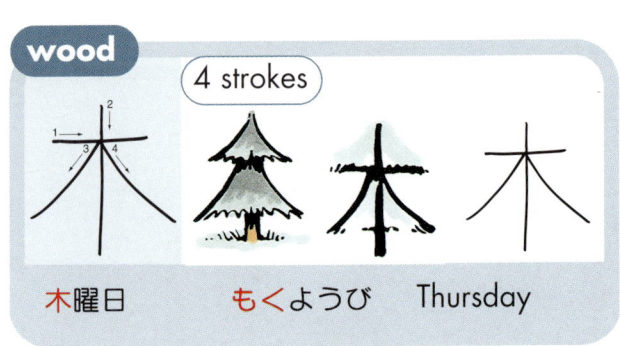

new reading — day, sun
4 strokes

日本	にほん	Japan
母の日	ははのひ	Mother's Day
日曜日	にちようび	Sunday

day of the week
18 strokes

日曜日　にちようび　Sunday

moon
4 strokes

月曜日　げつようび　Monday

fire
4 strokes

火曜日　かようび　Tuesday

water
4 strokes

水曜日　すいようび　Wednesday

wood
4 strokes

木曜日　もくようび　Thursday

metal
8 strokes

金曜日　きんようび　Friday

earth
3 strokes

土曜日　どようび　Saturday

うたいましょう！

日曜日も

1. (月) 月曜日は 学校の 日
   かぞくは おきます、6時に

   chorus:
   月、火、水、木、金、土
   月、火、水、木、金、土
   月、火、水、木、金、土

2. (火) 火曜日は 学校の 日
   おいしい あさごはんは 7時に

   くりかえし chorus

3. (水) 水曜日は 学校の 日
   学校に 行きます、8時に

   くりかえし chorus

4. (木) 木曜日は 学校の 日
   テニスの れんしゅうは 4時半に

   くりかえし chorus

5. (金) 金曜日は 学校の 日
   うちに かえります、5時半に

   くりかえし chorus

6. (土) 土曜日は スポーツの 日
   学校に 行きます、9時半に

   くりかえし chorus

7. (日) 日曜日は あさねぼうの 日
   わたしは おきます、12時に

   月、火、水、木、金、土
   (日) 日曜日も、日曜日も
   (日) 日曜日も、日曜日も

   くりかえし

What day is it?

- To ask what day of the week it is say きょうは 何曜日 ですか。
- To say what day it is say きょうは (day) です。

   きょうは 木曜日 です。
   Today is Thursday.

What day is it on?

- To ask what day something is on say (thing)は 何曜日 ですか。

   かんじの テストは 何曜日 ですか。
   What day is the kanji test (on)?

- To say what day something is on say (thing)は (day) です。

   かんじの テストは 金曜日 です。
   The kanji test is (on) Friday.

だい五か

口れんしゅう

きょうこ has a busy week ahead. Look at this page from her diary and you'll see what we mean. (We've given you a hand with reading the katakana words.)

月曜日	コンサート(ko n sa a to)の れんしゅう
火曜日	かいもの
水曜日	すいえい
木曜日	えい語の テスト(te su to)
金曜日	テニス(te ni su)の れんしゅう
土曜日	りつこの たんじょうび パーティー(pa a ti i)
日曜日	かいもの

たんご: たんじょうび — birthday

Warm-up

When you point to an entry in きょうこ's diary your partner will tell you what day it is for.

Talking seriously

Now ask your partner what day something is on. Be prepared to answer the same sort of question yourself. Here is an example of the sort of conversation you might have:

You: すいえいは 何曜日 ですか。
Partner: 水曜日 です。

Talking very seriously

If you think you're ready to branch out a bit, you and your partner could ask each other what きょうこ is planning to do on a particular day.

You: 水曜日に 何を しますか。
Partner: すいえいを します。

A visit to Hakone

Next time you're in Japan, take the two-hour train trip south from Tokyo and visit Hakone National Park. Hakone is one of Japan's most famous tourist spots because of its beautiful forests, mountains and lakes. But the real Hakone highlight is Mt Fuji (ふじさん), which you can see from various points along the tourist trail.

Another thing that makes the Hakone tourist trail special is the fact that you can travel around it on different types of transport, including bus, train, cable car and sailing ship. To keep costs down you should buy a Weekday Pass – but before you do, check the brochure to see which days it is valid for.

Hakone is also famous for its open-air art museum, with lots of great statues by world-famous sculptors. Time your visit there to take advantage of the free pass available to primary and junior high school students. Check the board to find out when it's available. (You're a 中学生.)

Will you be able to use your Hakone Weekday Pass and free entry to the open-air art museum on the same trip?

だい五か

Happy days!

You first met the Asano family in だい1か. In this section, Minako Asano introduces her family and tells us a little bit about each person in it.

Her presentation will provide you with all the fun of a serious reading challenge: it gathers together most of the language you have been working on in this book.

As you read, you can see Minako's plan. She tells us:

- each person's position in the family, their name and how old they are;
- what they're into and/or what they like.

She also makes a comment about the person or what they do.

Most importantly, Minako's presentation will inspire you to do something similar.
がんばって！

こんにちは！

『わたしの かぞく です』
by
あさの みなこ

わたしは みなこ です。10さい です。

わたしの かぞく です。
かぞくは 5人 です。
父と 母と あねと あにと わたし です。

お父さん、どうぞ。

父の ふじお です。父は 45さい です。
父は おいしい ケーキ(ke e ki) と コーヒー(ko o hi i) が すき です。しゅうまつに、父は よく ゴルフ(go ru fu) を します。

たんご	
つくります	makes
おわり	The end

だい五か

六十二

母 です。 なまえは みえこ です。41さい です。
母は あさごはんに さかなと ごはんを 食べます。
そして、コーヒー(ko o hi i)を のみます。おもしろい ですね。

④

あね です。なまえは さわこ です。
13さい です。 あねは りょうりが すき です。
あねの りょうりは おいしい です。
しゅうまつに、よく ケーキ(ke e ki)を つくります。
父と わたしは よく あねの ケーキ(ke e ki)を 食べます。

⑤

⑥

わたし です。
わたしは テレビ(te re bi)が 大すき です。
日曜日に よく 見ます。
そうじが すきじゃない です。

⑦

あにの まさる です。あには
15さい です。あにの へやを
見て ください。 あには
おんがくが すき です。よく
ギター(gi ta a)の れんしゅうを します。
うるさい です。

わたしの かぞくは
いい かぞく です！

おわり！

だい五か

六十三

63

Japanese-English

あ／a

あさごはん	breakfast
あさごはんに	for breakfast, at breakfast time
あさねぼう	sleepy head
あに	my big brother
あね	my big sister
あまり ...	not much
あまり すきじゃない	don't like much
ありがとう	thanks
ありがとう ございます	thank you

い／i

いい	good
いいえ	no
いきます、行きます	go
いただきます	(said before a meal)
いってきます	(said when you are leaving the house)
いってらっしゃい	(said when someone else is leaving the house)
いぬ	dog
いま	now
いもうと	my little sister
いもうとさん	your little sister

う／u

うさぎ	rabbit
うち	house, home
うま	horse
うるさい	noisy, annoying
うわあ！	Wow!

え／e

えいご、えい語	English
えいごの しゅくだい、えい語の しゅくだい	English homework
えっ！	Oh! (expression of surprise)
ええと ...	umm, aah

お／o

おいしい	yummy
おおきい、大きい	big
おかあさん、お母さん	Mum, mother
おかえりなさい	welcome home
おきます	get up
おじゃまします	don't mind me
おちゃ	green tea
おとうさん、お父さん	Dad, father
おとうと	my little brother
おとうとさん	your little brother
おはし	chopsticks
おふろ	Japanese-style bath
おにいさん	big brother, your big brother
おねえさん	big sister, your big sister
おもしろい	interesting
おやすみなさい	good night
おやつ	snack
おわり	The end
おんがく	music

か／ka, が／ga

かいます	buy
かいもの	shopping
かえります	go home
かぞく	my family
がっこう、学校	school
かめ	turtle
かようび、火曜日	Tuesday
かわいい	cute
がんばって！	Go for it! Hang in there!
がんばれ！	Go for it! Hang in there!

き／ki, ぎ／gi

ききます	listen
きたない	dirty
ぎゅうにゅう	milk
きゅうにん、九人	nine people
きんようび、金曜日	Friday

く／ku, ぐ／gu

くにん、九人	nine people

け／ke, げ／ge

げつようび、月曜日	Monday
げんかん	entrance (to a Japanese home)

こ／ko, ご／go

こうちゃ	tea
ごかぞく	your family
ごじゅうごふん、五十五分	fifty-five minutes
ごじゅっぷん、五十分	fifty minutes
ごちそうさま	thanks for the food
こどものひ、こどもの日	Children's Day
ごにん、五人	five people
この	this
このじは、何ですか	What is this hiragana? (How do you read this?)
ごはん	cooked rice, meal
ごふん、五分	five minutes
ごふんまえ、五分まえ	five minutes to ~
ごりょうしん	your parents
こわい	scary
こんにちは	hello, good afternoon
こんばんは	good evening

さ／sa

～さい	... years old
さかな	fish
さようなら	bye, goodbye
さんじゅうごふん、三十五分	thirty-five minutes
さんじゅっぷん、三十分	thirty minutes
さんにん、三人	three people

し／shi, じ／ji

～じ、～時	... o'clock
しごと	work
しずかに	Quiet! Shut up!
しずかにして	Be quiet!

64

しちにん、七人	seven people
します	do, play (games, sport)
じゃ	OK then
じゃんけん	paper, rock, scissors game
じゅうごふん、十五分	fifteen minutes
じゅうにん、十人	ten people
しゅうまつ	weekend
しゅくだい	homework
じゅっぷん、十分	ten minutes
じゅっぷんまえ、十分まえ	ten minutes to (the hour)

す／su

すいえい	swimming
すいようび、水曜日	Wednesday
すき	like
すきじゃない	don't like
すき ですか	Do you like it?
すごい	fantastic, amazing
すし	sushi
すみません	excuse me

そ／so

そうじ	cleaning
そして	And, And then
そうですね	It is, isn't it?

た／ta, だ／da

だいすき、大すき	like a lot, love
ただいま	I'm home!
たべます、食べます	eat
だれの〜	whose ...?
たんじょうび	birthday

ち／chi

ちいさい、小さい	small
ちち、父	my father
ちちのひ、父の日	Father's Day

つ／tsu

つくります	makes

て／te, で／de

でも	but

と／to, ど／do

と	and (to link two nouns)
ともだち	friend
どうしよう？！	What will I do?!
どうぞ	Here you are
どうぞ よろしく	Nice to meet you
どようび、土曜日	Saturday
とり	bird

な／na

ななにん、七人	seven people
なまえ	name
なに、何	what
なんじ、何時	what time?
なんじ ですか、何じ ですか	What time is it?
なんにん、何人	how many people?
なんようび、何曜日	what day?
なん ですか、何 ですか	What is it?

に／ni

〜に	at (a time); to (a place); for (breakfast etc)
にく	meat
にじゅうごふん、二十五分	twenty-five minutes
にじゅっぷん、二十分	twenty minutes
にちようび、日曜日	Sunday
にほんご、日本語	Japanese (language)
にほんごの しゅくだい、日本語の しゅくだい	Japanese homework
にほんごで、日本語で	in Japanese
にほん、日本	Japan
にんじゃ	a Ninja

ね／ne

ねこ	cat
ねずみ	mouse
ねます	go to bed

の／no

のみます	drink

は／ha, ば／ba

はい	yes
はちにん、八人	eight people
はは、母	my mother
ははのひ、母の日	Mother's Day
はやく	Hurry up!
ばんごはん	dinner
〜はん、〜半	half past ...

ひ／hi

ひとり、一人	one person

ふ／fu, ぶ／bu, ぷ／pu

ふたり、二人	two people
〜ふん／〜ぷん、〜分	... minutes
ふじさん	Mount Fuji

へ／he

へえ！	Really?!
へび	snake
へや	room

ほ／ho, ぼ／bo

ぼく	I, me (boy speaking)
ぼくの	my, mine (boy speaking)
ほんとう？	Really?!

ま／ma

まあまあ すき	It's OK
まえ	before, in front of
まんが	comic, cartoon

み／mi

みそしる	miso (soybean) soup
みて、見て	Look!

みなさん	everyone
みましょう、見ましょう	let's watch
みます、見ます	look, see, watch

も／mo
もくようび、木曜日	Thursday

よ／yo
よく	often
よにん、四人	four people
よみます	read
よんじゅうごふん、四十五分	forty-five minutes
よんじゅっぷん、四十分	forty minutes
よんで	read

り／ri, りょ／ryo
りょうしん	my parents
りょうり	cooking, cuisine

れ／re
れんしゅう	practice, training

ろ／ro
ろくにん、六人	six people

わ／wa
わたし	I, me
わたしの	my, mine

Katakana words
bando バンド	band
biggu burazaa ビッグ・ブラザー	Big Brother (television show)
chippusu チップス	chips (crisps)
chokoreeto チョコレート	chocolate
gitaa ギター	guitar
gorufu booru ゴルフボール	golf ball
gorufu ゴルフ	golf
guruupu グループ	group
jogingu ジョギング	jogging
juusu ジュース	juice
karaoke カラオケ	karaoke
keeki ケーキ	cake
konsaato コンサート	concert
koohii コーヒー	coffee
kurasu クラス	class
piza ピザ	pizza
purezento プレゼント	present
sakkaa サッカー	soccer
shiriaru シリアル	cereal
teikuauto テイクアウト	takeaway (food)
tenisu テニス	tennis
terebi テレビ	television
terebi geemu テレビ・ゲーム	video game
tesuto テスト	test
toosuto トースト	toast

English–Japanese

A
aah, umm	ええと…
amazing, fantastic	すごい
and (to link two nouns)	と
And, And then	そして
at (a time)	〜に

B
band	バンド bando
bath (Japanese-style)	おふろ
before, in front of	まえ
big	おおきい、大きい
bird	とり
birthday	たんじょうび
breakfast	あさごはん
for breakfast, at breakfast time	あさごはんに
brother	
big brother, your big brother	おにいさん
my big brother	あに
my little brother	おとうと
your little brother	おとうとさん
but	でも
buy	かいます
bye, goodbye	さようなら

C
cake	ケーキ keeki
card	カード kaado
cartoon, comic	まんが
cat	ねこ
cereal	シリアル shiriaru
Children's Day	こどものひ、こどもの日
chips (crisps)	チップス chippusu
chocolate	チョコレート chokoreeto
chopsticks	おはし
class	クラス kurasu
cleaning	そうじ
coffee	コーヒー koohii
concert	コンサート konsaato
cooking, cuisine	りょうり
cute	かわいい

D
Dad, your father	おとうさん、お父さん
dinner	ばんごはん
dirty	きたない
do, play (games, sport)	します
dog	いぬ
don't mind me	おじゃまします
drink	のみます

E
eat	たべます、食べます
eight people	はちにん、八人
(the) end	おわり

English	えいご、えい語
entrance (to a Japanese home)	げんかん
everyone	みなさん
excuse me	すみません

F

family	
my family	かぞく
your family	ごかぞく
fantastic, amazing	すごい
father	
Dad, your father	おとうさん、お父さん
Father's Day	ちちのひ、父の日
my father	ちち、父
fifteen minutes	じゅうごふん、十五分
fifty minutes	ごじゅっぷん、五十分
fifty-five minutes	ごじゅうごふん、五十五分
fish	さかな
five	
five minutes	ごふん、五分
five minutes to ~	ごふんまえ
five people	ごにん、五人
five points	ごてん
for breakfast, at breakfast time	あさごはんに
forty minutes	よんじゅっぷん、四十分
forty-five minutes	よんじゅうごふん、四十五分
four	
four people	よにん、四人
four points	よんてん
Friday	きんようび、金曜日
friend	ともだち

G

get up	おきます
go	いきます、行きます
Go for it! Hang in there!	がんばって！がんばれ！
go home	かえります
go to bed	ねます
golf ball	ゴルフボール gorufubooru
golf	ゴルフ gorufu
good	いい
good afternoon, hello	こんにちは
goodbye, bye	さようなら
good evening	こんばんは
good night	おやすみなさい
green tea	おちゃ
group	グループ guruupu
guitar	ギター gitaa

H

half past ...	～はん、～半
Hang in there! Go for it!	がんばって！がんばれ！
hello, good afternoon	こんにちは
here you are	どうぞ

homework	しゅくだい
English homework	えいごの しゅくだい、えい語の しゅくだい
Japanese homework	にほんごの しゅくだい、日本語の しゅくだい
horse	うま
house, home	うち
how many people?	なんにん、何人
hurry up	はやく

I

It is, isn't it?	そうですね
It's OK	まあまあ すき
I, me	わたし
I, me (boy speaking)	ぼく
interesting	おもしろい
I'm home	ただいま

J

Japan	にほん、日本
Japanese (language)	にほんご、日本語
in Japanese	にほんごで、日本語で
jogging	ジョギング jogingu
juice	ジュース juusu
junior high school student	ちゅうがくせい、中学生

K

karaoke	カラオケ karaoke

L

let's watch	みましょう、見ましょう
like	すき
Do you like it?	すき ですか
don't like	すきじゃない
It's OK	まあまあ すき
like a lot, love	だいすき、大すき
don't like much	あまり すきじゃない
listen	ききます
look, see, watch	みます、見ます
Look!	みて、見て

M

make, to make	つくります
meal, cooked rice	ごはん
meat	にく
milk	ぎゅうにゅう
minutes	～ふん／～ぷん、～分
miso (soybean) soup	みそしる
Monday	げつようび、月曜日
mother, Mum	
Mother's Day	ははのひ、母の日
mum, your mother	おかあさん、お母さん
my mother	はは、母
Mount Fuji	ふじさん
mouse	ねずみ
music	おんがく
my, mine	わたしの

my, mine (boy speaking)	ぼくの

N

name	なまえ
nice to meet you	どうぞ よろしく
nine people	きゅうにん、九人；くにん、九人
Ninja	にんじゃ
no	いいえ
noisy, annoying	うるさい
not much	あまり …

O

often	よく
OK	
It's OK	まあまあ すき
OK then	じゃ
o'clock	〜じ、〜時
one person	ひとり、一人

P

paper, rock, scissors game	じゃんけん
(my) parents	りょうしん
(your) parents	ごりょうしん
pizza	ピザ piza
play (games, sport), do	します
practice, training	れんしゅう
present, gift	プレゼント purezento

Q

Quiet! Shut up!	しずかに
Be quiet!	しずかにして

R

rabbit	うさぎ
rice (cooked), meal	ごはん
read	よみます
read	よんで
Really?!	へえ！；ほんとう？
room	へや

S

Saturday	どようび、土曜日
scary	こわい
school	がっこう、学校
see, look, watch,	みます、見ます
seven people	しちにん、七人；ななにん、七人
shopping	かいもの
Shut up!, Quiet!	しずかに
sister	
big sister, your big sister	おねえさん
my big sister	あね
my little sister	いもうと
your little sister	いもうとさん
six people	ろくにん、六人
sleepy head	あさねぼう
small	ちいさい、小さい
snack	おやつ
soccer	サッカー sakkaa

sport	スポーツ supootsu
Sunday	にちようび、日曜日
sushi	すし
swimming	すいえい

T

takeaway (food)	テイクアウト teikuauto
tea	こうちゃ
television	テレビ terebi
ten	
ten minutes	じゅっぷん、十分
ten minutes to (the hour)	じゅっぷんまえ、十分まえ
ten people	じゅうにん、十人
tennis	テニス tenisu
test	テスト tesuto
thank you	ありがとう ございます
thanks	ありがとう
thanks for the food	ごちそうさま
thirty minutes	さんじゅっぷん、三十分
thirty-five minutes	さんじゅうごふん、三十五分
this	この
three people	さんにん、三人
Thursday	もくようび、木曜日
toast	トースト toosuto
Tuesday	かようび、火曜日
turtle	かめ
twenty minutes	にじゅっぷん、二十分
twenty-five minutes	にじゅうごふん、二十五分
two people	ふたり、二人

U

umm, aah	ええと …

W

watch, look, see	みます、見ます
let's watch	みましょう、見ましょう
Wednesday	すいようび、水曜日
weekend	しゅうまつ
welcome home	おかえりなさい
what	なに、何
what day?	なんようび、何曜日
What is it?	なん ですか、何 ですか
what time?	なんじ、何時
What time is it?	なんじ ですか、何時 ですか
What will I do?!	どうしよう？！
whose …?	だれの〜
work	しごと
Wow!	うわあ！

Y

… years old	〜さい
yes	はい
yummy	おいしい